North American Birds

A BUR OAK BOOK

HOLLY CARVER, SERIES EDITOR

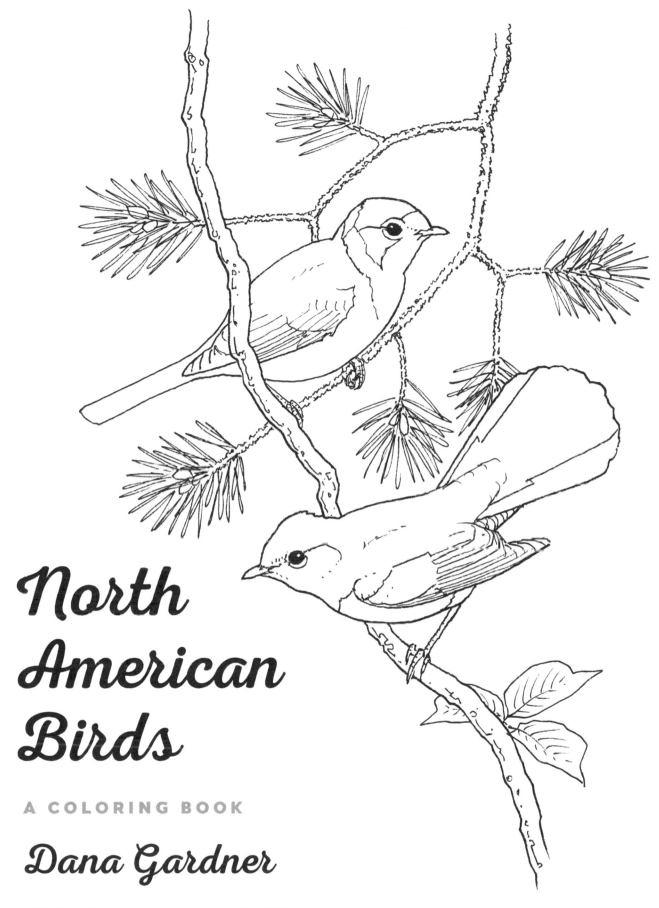

North American Birds

A COLORING BOOK

Dana Gardner

UNIVERSITY OF IOWA PRESS, IOWA CITY

University of Iowa Press, Iowa City 52242

Copyright © 2017 by the University of Iowa Press

www.uipress.uiowa.edu

Printed in the United States of America

Design by April Leidig

The University of Iowa Press is a member of Green Press Initiative and is committed to preserving natural resources.

Printed on acid-free paper

ISBN: 978-1-60938-520-0

Bird illustrations on the previous pages depict evening grosbeaks, red-faced warbler (top), and painted redstart (bottom); illustration on the facing page shows a blue grosbeak.

North American Birds

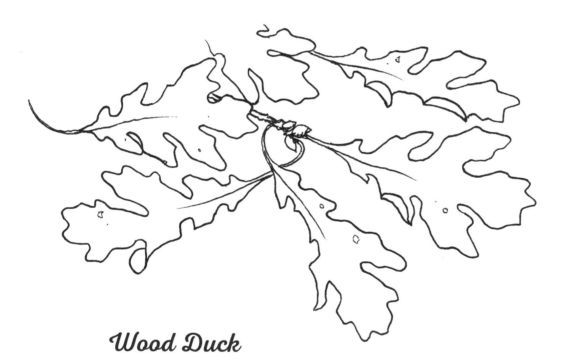

Wood Duck

The highly ornamental male wood duck presents an unforgettable sight along the wooded edges of lakes and rivers. But wood ducks are shy and unobtrusive birds, and I count myself lucky if I see them a few times every spring. The female makes her nest in a hole of a tree, sometimes very high up. When the newly hatched ducklings are ready to leave the nest, they tumble out of the hole and fall unharmed to the ground, ready to follow their mother off to feeding grounds.

Atlantic Puffin

Many people know what a puffin is, but few have actually seen this comical bird with its big colorful bill. It nests in colonies on cliffs around the North Atlantic and spends the winter out on the open ocean.

Brown Pelican

The picturesque brown pelican is strictly a coastal bird. A victim of DDT poisoning, it nearly disappeared in the 1970s and 1980s. Now its population has rebounded, and groups can be seen flying in single file, interspersed with spectacular dives to catch fish, along all coastal areas of the country.

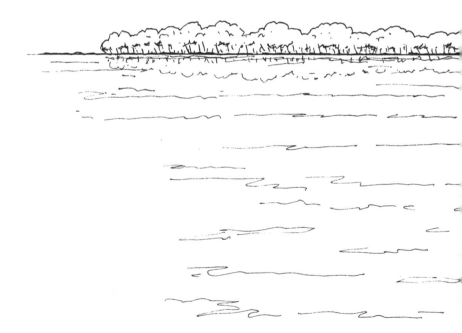

American Kestrel

The colorful little kestrel, formerly called the sparrow hawk, is our smallest falcon. Grasshoppers and other insects make up the bulk of its diet, but it will occasionally take the unwary rodent or small bird. I often see them perched on telephone wires in rural areas, their sharp eyes searching for prey.

Great Horned Owl

This large owl is common throughout the country in many different habitats, but because it is nocturnal, it is seldom seen. If you are walking in the woods and hear a group of various birds making a lot of noise, it is often because they have found a roosting owl. They view the owl as a dangerous threat — it *is* a powerful hunter — and sound the alarm so that all creatures nearby will know its whereabouts.

Mountain Quail

The mountain quail is another strikingly patterned bird that people seldom see. Though fairly common, it is shy and often sits motionless in the thick undergrowth of mountains in the far West.

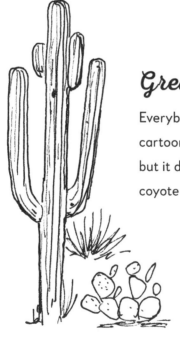

Greater Roadrunner

Everybody knows the crafty roadrunner who always outwits the coyote in cartoons. The real bird lacks the colorful plumes of its cartoon counterpart, but it does share its lively manner and speedy deportment. I doubt if a coyote ever catches one.

Wild Turkey

At the beginning of the twentieth century, the long-legged wild turkey had been overhunted and was a scarce bird. Reintroduced to its former range as well as to new areas, it is now common in many parts of the country. I never saw a wild turkey when I was growing up in southeastern Minnesota, but now it is an abundant bird there. Unlike the often disparaged barnyard turkey, the wild turkey is an intelligent and wary creature. It feeds on a large variety of vegetable material, but acorns are a favorite food item.

American Bittern

If you have never seen an American bittern, it is probably because it has seen you first. At any sign of danger, this solitary bird slowly assumes a vertical posture and freezes, then disappears among the reeds and cattails of its marshy home.

Ruddy Turnstone

The robust ruddy turnstone, true to its name, uses its oddly upturned beak to turn over rocks, shells, and shoreline debris in search of food. It nests in the High Arctic but migrates throughout the country and spends the winter months along our coasts.

Carolina Parakeet

The bright green Carolina parakeet with its yellow head and red-orange face was the only parrot native to the United States. Heavily persecuted for foraging on crops, it passed into extinction, along with the passenger pigeon, early in the twentieth century.

Belted Kingfisher

There are many kinds of kingfishers around the world, but the stocky belted kingfisher with its rattling call is the only one commonly found throughout the United States. It is often seen perched above water, intently searching for small fish beneath the surface. Upon sighting something suitable, it plunges headfirst into the water to seize it.

Elegant Trogon

The many distinctive trogons are native to tropical areas. Only in Arizona can you hope to see a trogon north of the border. Many birdwatchers search for elegant trogons along the sycamore-lined canyons in the mountains of southeastern Arizona.

Acorn Woodpecker

These clown-faced birds of the West and Southwest live in colonies. They drill large numbers of small holes in a dead tree, called a granary tree, and wedge an acorn into each hole. This stored food is eaten in the lean winter months and the following spring.

Yellow-bellied Sapsucker
Ruby-throated Hummingbird

Yellow-bellied sapsuckers drill rows of little holes in birches and other trees in order to feed on the sap that wells up and the insects that are attracted to it. In an early spring cold snap, hummingbirds will take advantage of this food source if flowers are still scarce.

Northern Flicker

This large and colorful woodpecker has a lot going on with its plumage: spots, stripes, blotches of various colors and shapes. A common bird of open woodlands, it can often be seen on the ground foraging for ants.

Cliff Swallow

Cliff swallows have adapted well to humans' changes to the environment. Nesting in colonies, they readily build their jug-shaped mud nests under bridges and large culverts. In southeastern Minnesota, I would often see colonies of these birds nesting under the eaves of large barns.

Scissor-tailed Flycatcher

The southern Great Plains is the summer home of this striking bird.
It is often seen perched on roadside fences and telephone lines. It sallies
out after insects, flaring its long tail streamers and displaying the salmon
pink on its shoulders and underwings.

American Robin

This conspicuous and familiar bird is common in suburban backyards as well as farmlands and forests. Its warbled dawn song is a sure sign of spring. The spot-breasted youngsters chase their parents across lawns, clamoring for food.

Eastern Bluebird

Bluebirds were rare when I was growing up in rural Minnesota.
Thanks to programs that encouraged people to put up nest boxes,
the population has recovered, and this elegant bird is now a
common sight along rural roads.

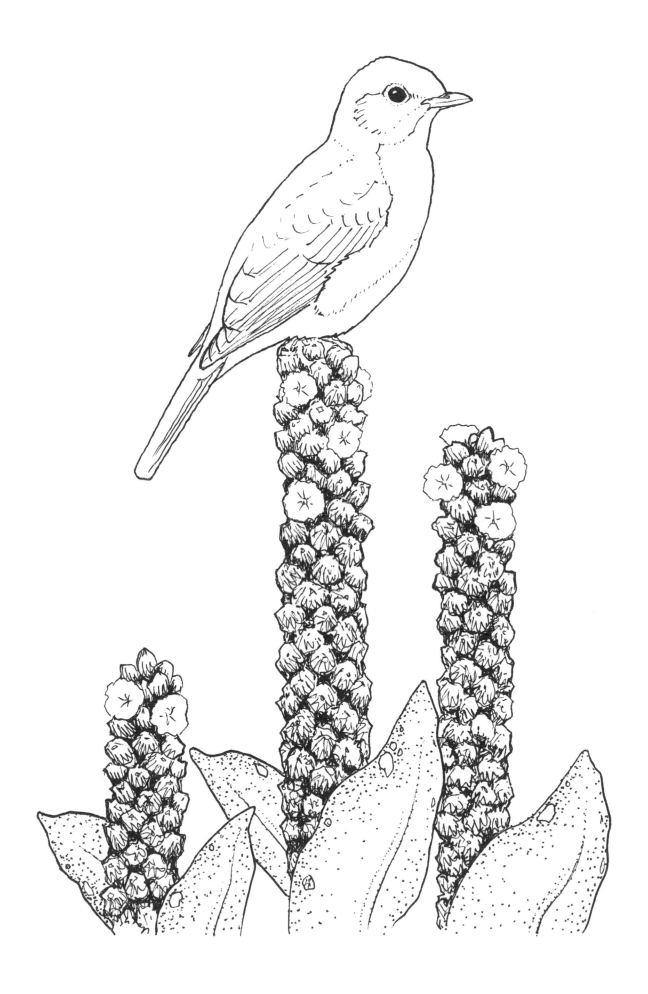

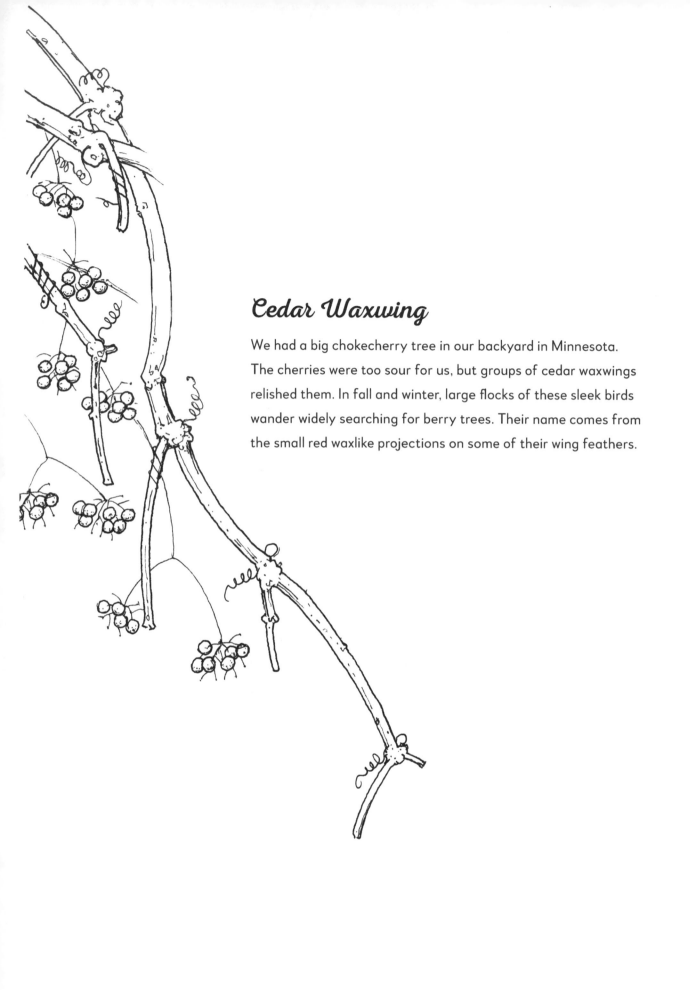

Cedar Waxwing

We had a big chokecherry tree in our backyard in Minnesota. The cherries were too sour for us, but groups of cedar waxwings relished them. In fall and winter, large flocks of these sleek birds wander widely searching for berry trees. Their name comes from the small red waxlike projections on some of their wing feathers.

Horned Lark

There are a lot of larks in Africa and Asia, but the horned lark is
the only representative of its family native to the Western Hemisphere.
In the winter, nomadic flocks of larks can be seen traveling around
open fields and barren areas.

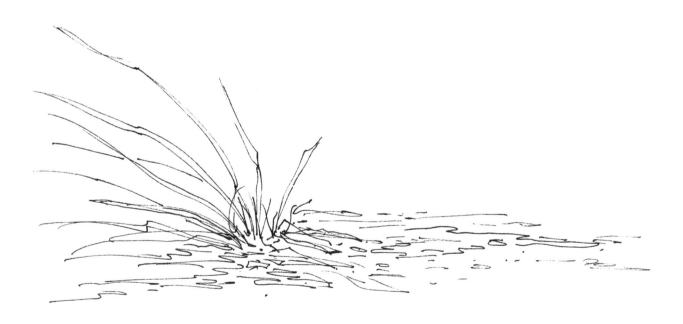

Blue Jay

The bold and raucous blue jay, common throughout eastern North America,
readily visits bird feeders for a variety of food. At my Minnesota bird feeder,
the smaller birds would scatter when a blue jay flew in. It is also not above
plundering other birds' nests and devouring eggs and small chicks.

Green Jay

Though most jays in North America are clad in various shades of blue, the dazzling green jay of more tropical areas resides in southern Texas. In the lower Rio Grande Valley, it is common in wooded areas and parks and sometimes comes to picnic tables looking for food scraps.

Cape May Warbler
Blackburnian Warbler
Bay-breasted Warbler

Colorful warblers such as the (top to bottom) Cape May, Blackburnian, and bay-breasted rush north in the spring to nest at their earliest opportunity. Birdwatchers crane their necks to spot the migrating birds in the treetops, resulting in the achy malady known as warbler neck. In Minnesota in mid-May, we hoped for a twenty-warbler day, when it might be possible to see more than twenty species of migrating warblers. And this resulted in a bad case of warbler neck.

Red-winged Blackbird
Yellow-headed Blackbird

The assertive red-winged blackbird (right) is a familiar and widespread bird. A pair seems to inhabit every grassy field in the countryside. The handsome yellow-headed blackbird (left) is more strictly confined to marshy areas of western and midwestern states. Both species congregate in the winter into large wandering flocks.

Western Meadowlark

There is a western meadowlark and an eastern meadowlark, and both of them can be found throughout the Midwest. They look similar to each other, but their songs are very different. Meadowlarks frequent prairies and other grassy expanses. In my youth they were abundant, and I often saw them singing from the tops of telephone poles. Nowadays they are noticeably scarcer. Perhaps modern farming practices leave fewer undisturbed grassy areas for them.

Dickcissel

The dickcissel, which resembles a miniature meadowlark, is a nomadic
wanderer of northern and midwestern grasslands. I remember seeing the
birds in the overgrown fields of Minnesota one year, then finding them
entirely absent the following year.

American Goldfinch

The agile goldfinch likes thistles. It nests late in the summer when it can incorporate the fluff of thistle seeds into its nest. And in winter, flocks of goldfinches will visit bird feeders that offer thistle seed. Their winter plumage is much drabber than their colorful spring plumage.

Northern Cardinal

Seven states have chosen the attractive northern cardinal,
a common bird throughout the eastern United States, as their
state bird. It was one of my favorite birds at my Minnesota
bird feeder. The availability of food, as well as warming winters,
has enabled the cardinal to extend its range northward in
recent decades, and it can now be found well into Canada.

Painted Bunting

The male painted bunting sports a spectacular array of bright colors, but it is surprisingly hard to see as it skulks in brushy and overgrown areas of southern and southeastern states. You can hope to see the multicolored male in the spring as it perches in the open to sing its song.

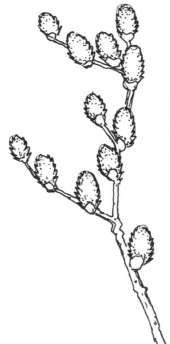

Rose-breasted Grosbeak

In Minnesota, I loved seeing the rose-breasted grosbeak arrive in the spring and hearing its warbling song. This meant that spring had finally arrived, and soon the leaves would grow bigger, making the bird much harder to see.

Eastern Towhee

This large and colorful sparrow, formerly called the rufous-sided towhee, is common in wooded areas throughout the East and Midwest, but it is not easy to see. I often heard its distinctive "drink your tea" song in the Minnesota woods, but I seldom saw the bird.

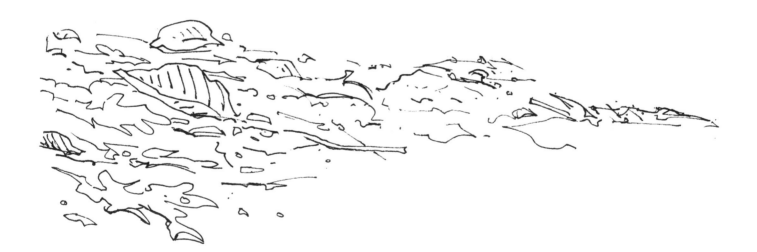

Baltimore Oriole

This bird was given its name because it sports the colors of the coat of arms of the seventeenth-century Lord Baltimore. These are common birds in the East, and their baglike hanging nests are often seen at the tips of drooping branches of shade trees in urban areas.